Mrs. Carter's
BUTTERFLY
GARDEN

STEVE RICH

NSTA Kids
National Science Teachers Association

Arlington, Virginia

National Science Teachers Association

Claire Reinburg, Director
Wendy Rubin, Managing Editor
Andrew Cooke, Senior Editor
Amanda O'Brien, Associate Editor
Amy America, Book Acquisitions Coordinator

ART AND DESIGN
Will Thomas Jr., Director
Joe Butera, Cover, Interior Design

PRINTING AND PRODUCTION
Catherine Lorrain, Director

NATIONAL SCIENCE TEACHERS ASSOCIATION
David L. Evans, Executive Director
David Beacom, Publisher

1840 Wilson Blvd., Arlington, VA 22201
www.nsta.org/store
For customer service inquiries, please call 800-277-5300.

Lexile® measure: AD 1120L

NSTA is committed to publishing material that promotes the best in inquiry-based science education. However, conditions of actual use may vary, and the safety procedures and practices described in this book are intended to serve only as a guide. Additional precautionary measures may be required. NSTA and the authors do not warrant or represent that the procedures and practices in this book meet any safety code or standard of federal, state, or local regulations. NSTA and the authors disclaim any liability for personal injury or damage to property arising out of or relating to the use of this book, including any of the recommendations, instructions, or materials contained therein.

Library of Congress Cataloging-in-Publication Data
Rich, Steve, 1962- author.
  Mrs. Carter's butterfly garden / by Steve Rich.
      pages cm
  Audience: K to grade 3.
  ISBN 978-1-941316-08-5 (pbk.) -- ISBN 978-1-941316-93-1 (e-book) 1. Butterfly gardening--Georgia--Plains--Juvenile literature. 2. Butterfly gardens--Georgia--Plains--Juvenile literature. 3. Carter, Rosalynn--Juvenile literature. I. Title. II. Title: Butterfly garden.
  QL544.6.R53 2014
  638'.578909758--dc23
                                        2014033832

Cataloging-in-Publication Data are also available from the Library of Congress for the e-book.
e-LCCN: 2014035257

Dedicated with admiration

to former First Lady

Rosalynn Carter,

for her commitment to making

the world a better place for so many people

and for so warmly and graciously welcoming butterflies and me

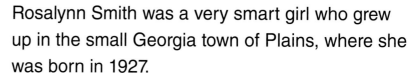

Rosalynn Smith was a very smart girl who grew up in the small Georgia town of Plains, where she was born in 1927.

She loved the colorful zinnias, petunias, and other flowers that her mother planted in the front yard of their traditional, white wood house.

Like many rural Georgia families, the Smiths had a milk cow. Young Rosalynn's father told her to pull up the milkweed growing wild along the fence because it made the cow's milk bitter. She didn't know then that one day she would plant milkweed to help another animal. She also loved to read, and she was an excellent student, graduating high school at the top of her class.

After finishing college, Rosalynn married another Plains native, Jimmy Carter. She first left Georgia as a Navy wife to travel wherever her husband was stationed. When her husband became governor of Georgia, Mrs. Rosalynn Carter became first lady of the state, and when he later became the 39th president of the United States (1977–1981), she became first lady of the entire nation.

First Lady is the title given to the wife of a state's governor or of the president of the United States. During their years in the Navy and political office, the Carters lived in places such as Georgia, Virginia, Connecticut, California, and Washington, D.C. Then, after many years of public service, President and Mrs. Carter returned home to Plains, Georgia.

Like many former presidential families, the Carters continue to live in their home but have granted it to the National Park Service, so it is a designated National Historic Site, and the park rangers help take care of the plants and grounds. As plans were made to plant a garden in front of Mrs. Carter's home, she wanted to make certain the garden would benefit the environment. Just as when she was a young girl, she turned to reading. She found out about a special kind of garden that has everything a butterfly needs. She also learned that human activity has destroyed many habitats for butterflies.

In a butterfly garden, there are plants with flowers that have sweet nectar that a butterfly can taste with its feet before drinking through its strawlike proboscis. There are also *host plants* on which butterflies lay eggs. Caterpillars hatch from these eggs and then spend their time eating leaves all day.

Mrs. Carter knew farmers around the town of Plains had crops that needed flying pollinators. After all, she and her husband had run the family peanut business before Jimmy's political career. What if she had a garden that would attract pollinators to the area?

The spot in front of Mrs. Carter's house was the right kind of sunny space.

She wanted most to provide a habitat for monarch butterflies, so she planted some milkweed, the host plant for this special migrating butterfly.

Mrs. Carter recalled that when she was a girl, her father had told her to pull up the milkweed to prevent the cow's milk from being bitter. That same bitterness protects the monarch caterpillar and butterfly by making them poisonous to predators such as birds.

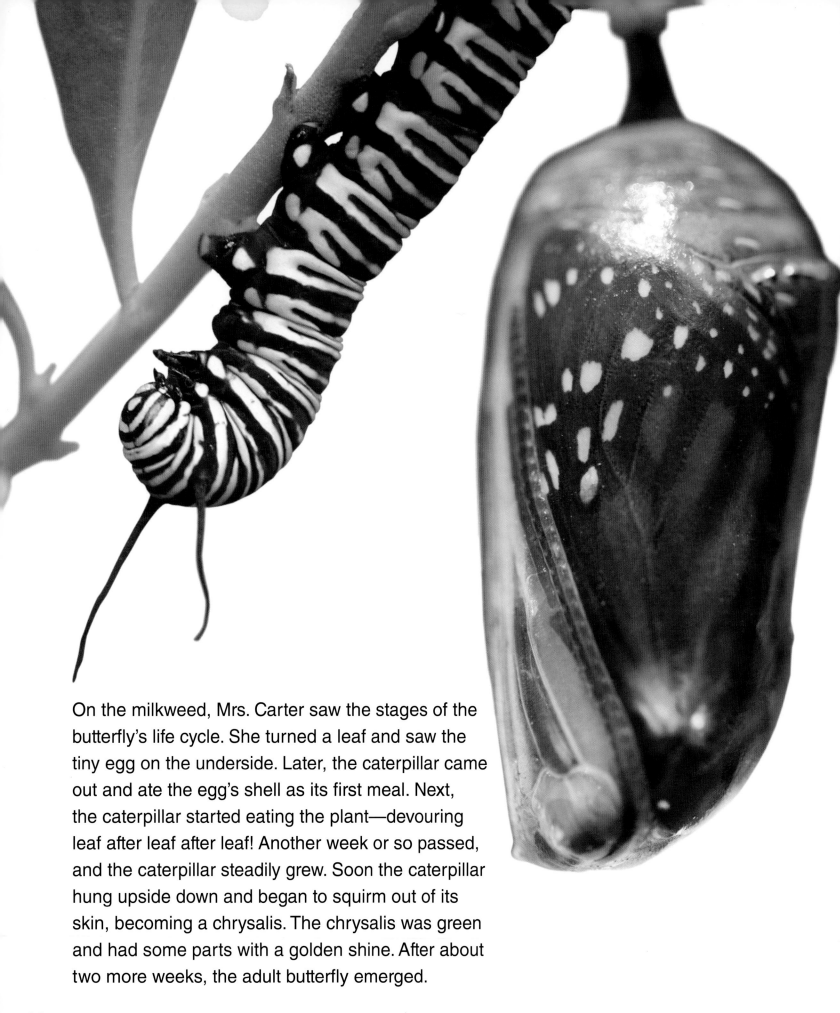

On the milkweed, Mrs. Carter saw the stages of the butterfly's life cycle. She turned a leaf and saw the tiny egg on the underside. Later, the caterpillar came out and ate the egg's shell as its first meal. Next, the caterpillar started eating the plant—devouring leaf after leaf after leaf! Another week or so passed, and the caterpillar steadily grew. Soon the caterpillar hung upside down and began to squirm out of its skin, becoming a chrysalis. The chrysalis was green and had some parts with a golden shine. After about two more weeks, the adult butterfly emerged.

Just as she had done all her life, Mrs. Carter wanted to share her work.

She wanted people to know about her garden when they came from all over to visit the Jimmy Carter National Historic Site in Plains.

So, she decided to have several gardens all along a special trail where visitors could see butterflies such as monarchs, swallowtails, skippers, Gulf fritillaries, and many other species. This would allow visitors to learn about how they can also plant gardens that provide habitats for monarch butterflies and other pollinators.

Local people helped. They planted more gardens at Plains High School, the Jimmy Carter Boyhood Farm, the Plains Welcome Center, and even downtown Plains.

18

Just as Mrs. Carter traveled around the country and the world throughout her life, the monarch butterfly travels in a seasonal migration. The butterflies fly south from Canada to places throughout the United States.

When it's cold they head to their winter destination, Mexico! In Mexico, they are dormant for several months. When the weather gets warm, they become active again.

In the spring, they start flying north. They mate and lay eggs. A new generation of butterflies comes back to the United States, and some stop in the garden at Mrs. Carter's home. There, they find the familiar plants and flowers that make up the butterfly habitat.

The butterflies also find special *puddling* pans where they can drink water through their proboscises, taking in minerals from the rocks and soil.

Mrs. Carter knows that world travelers can be refreshed with all they need in a small south Georgia town. It is her hope that the butterflies will find their way to her garden and have all the plants they need for many years to come.

She also hopes that people will find their way to Plains to learn about how two young people from this small town made it all the way to the White House as president and first lady—a different type of journey, but one with just as many challenges as the migrating butterflies face.

Glossary

Caterpillar
the wormlike, early stage of a butterfly's life when it first hatches from an egg

Chrysalis
the stage of a butterfly life cycle between the caterpillar and the adult butterfly

Crops
plants that grow food such as peanuts, beans, potatoes, or onions

First Lady
the wife of the president of the United States or a state's governor

Habitat
the natural environment of an animal or plant that contains all it needs to survive

Host Plant
the plant on which a butterfly lays its eggs so the caterpillars can eat its leaves

Migration
the movement of animals from one place to another, usually with the changing weather of the seasons

Milkweed
the host plant of the monarch butterfly

Monarch Butterfly
an orange-and-black butterfly known for its annual migration

Nectar
the sweet liquid inside a flower that butterflies like to drink

Pollinator
any animal that moves pollen from one plant to another, such as butterflies, bees, and birds

President
the elected leader of the United States of America

Proboscis
a tubelike structure through which a butterfly drinks

Swallowtail
a variety of butterflies with "tails" on each wing (The Eastern Tiger Swallowtail is the official state butterfly of Georgia.)

Additional Information for Parents and Teachers

Related Web Resources

The Rosalynn Carter Butterfly Trail,
Jimmy Carter NHS Education Program
www.jimmycarter.info/CarterButterflyTrail.htm

First Ladies
www.whitehouse.gov/about/first-ladies

Jimmy Carter Presidential Library and
Museum
www.jimmycarterlibrary.gov

Jimmy Carter National Historic Site,
Plains, Georgia
www.nps.gov/jica

Journey North
www.learner.org/jnorth

Monarch Watch
www.monarchwatch.org

Plains, Georgia
www.plainsgeorgia.com

If you are a parent or teacher sharing this book with young people, you might consider extending the experience with the following activities:

- Create a butterfly garden at your home or school with native plants that are comparable to those Mrs. Carter used in her garden.

- Help your children trace the migration of monarch butterflies and other animals on a map of North America.

- Tag migrating monarch butterflies in the program sponsored by Monarch Watch.

- Use a field guide or online resources to find out what butterflies are native to your area.

- Encourage kids to read about the importance of pollinators such as butterflies, bees, and birds.

- Help young people learn about the lives and service of President Jimmy Carter and Mrs. Rosalynn Carter using some of the web resources listed at left.

The Plants of the Rosalynn Carter Butterfly Trail

The author provided this list to Mrs. Carter when she started her butterfly garden project.

1. **Host Plants for the Monarch Butterfly**

   a. Milkweed*

   b. Butterfly Weed

2. **Host Plants for the Swallowtail Butterfly**

   a. Parsley (fall/winter)

   b. Dill (spring/summer)

   c. Fennel*

3. **Nectar Plants for Butterflies (Flowering Plants)**

   a. Annuals—Verbena, Zinnias, Marigolds

   b. Perennials—Black-eyed Susan, Goldenrod, Purple Coneflower

*Plants marked with an asterisk are considered to be invasive or a nuisance in some states. Gardeners are encouraged to use plants that are noninvasive and native to their region. None of the plants on this list appears on Georgia's list of invasive species, which is kept by the Georgia Exotic Plant Pest Council.

The Monarch Butterfly Life Cycle on Milkweed

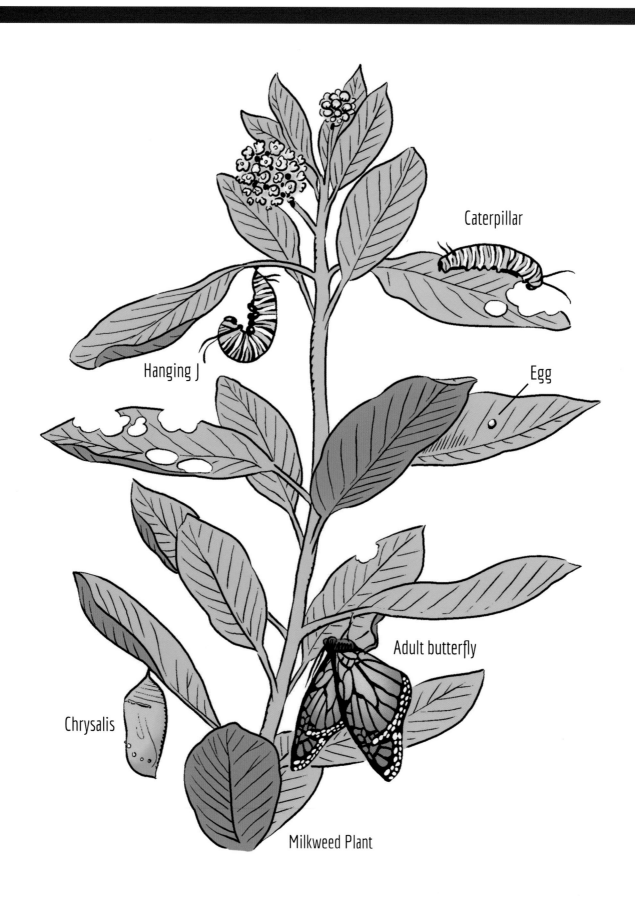

Caterpillar

Hanging J

Egg

Adult butterfly

Chrysalis

Milkweed Plant

About the Author

Steve Rich has been a science educator in Georgia for many years, with a particular interest in school gardens and teaching about butterflies. He is also the author of two NSTA Press books on teaching science outdoors. Steve was previously a state science specialist, and it was his former employer (the Georgia Department of Education) that connected him to the project in Plains because of his experience in butterfly gardening at schools. Another state education specialist stationed in Plains spearheaded the effort to establish the butterfly gardens for Mrs. Carter. Since first meeting with

Mrs. Carter in February 2013, Steve has visited Plains periodically, sharing plants, suggestions, and ideas to further the cause of providing habitats for butterflies and encouraging families and schools to visit the Rosalynn Carter Butterfly Trail.

About the Photographs

Painted Lady Butterflies

ThinkStock

Mrs. Carter

The Carter Center

Smith Family Home

Brian Becnel

Young Rosalynn Smith

Jimmy Carter Presidential
Library and Museum

Flowers in Plains

Brian Becnel

Milkweed (*Asclepias curassavica*) in Plains

Brian Becnel

Downtown Plains

Brian Becnel

Campaign Headquarters

Brian Becnel

Plains Welcome Sign

Brian Becnel

Silver-spotted Skipper

Brian Becnel

Plains Welcome Center Garden

Brian Becnel

Gulf Fritillary

Brian Becnel

Carter Farm Field

Brian Becnel

Swallowtail Caterpillar

Brian Becnel

Carter Boyhood Farm

Brian Becnel

Sulphur Butterfly

Brian Becnel

Monarch on *Buddleia*

Brian Becnel

Native Butterfly Weed (*Asclepias tuberosa*)

Brian Becnel

CONTINUED...

About the Photographs

Milkweed (*Asclepias curassavica*)

Brian Becnel

Monarch Caterpillar

ThinkStock

Monarch Chrysalis

Tom Uhlman

Adult Monarch

Tom Uhlman

Downtown Plains

Brian Becnel

Fritillary on *Lantana*

Brian Becnel

National Park Ranger

Brian Becnel

Farm Butterfly Garden

Brian Becnel

Fritillary on Marigold (*Calendula*)

Brian Becnel

Monarch on Gayfeather (*Liatris mucronata*)

Tom Uhlman

Monarch on Goldenrod (*Asteraceae solidago*)

Tom Uhlman

Puddling Pan

Brian Becnel

Welcome Center Sign

Brian Becnel

Butterfly Trail Sign

Brian Becnel

Jimmy and Rosalynn Carter

Jimmy Carter Presidential
Library and Museum

Rosalynn and Jimmy Carter

Stephen Cord, The Carter Center

The White House

ThinkStock

Dill and Parsley

ThinkStock

CONTINUED...

About the Photographs

Yellow *Rudbeckia*

ThinkStock

Calendula

ThinkStock

Carters and the Author

Conni Crittenden

**The Monarch Butterfly Life Cycle
on Milkweed**

Rich 2010

The Author

Ward Pix

Resources

Carter, J. 2001. *An hour before daylight*. New York: Simon & Schuster.

Carter, R. 1984, 1994. *First Lady from Plains*. Boston, MA: Houghton-Mifflin.

Georgia Exotic Plant Pest Council. *www.gaeppc.org/list.cfm*

National Research Council (NRC). 2012. *A framework for K–12 science education: Practices, crosscutting concepts, and core ideas*. Washington, DC: National Academies Press.

NGSS Lead States. 2013. *Next Generation Science Standards: For states, by states*. Washington, DC: National Academies Press. *www.nextgenscience.org/next-generation-science-standards.*

Rich, S. 2010. *Outdoor science: A practical guide*. Arlington, VA: NSTA Press.